UNCLE DANIEL IS A SYSTEMS ENGINEER

Anita Rowe Stafford

Published by Laughing Ladybug Press

UNCLE DANIEL IS A SYSTEMS ENGINEER

First edition. August 7, 2022.

Written by Anita Rowe Stafford.

This book is dedicated to all Systems Engineers, especially Uncle Daniel and his friend, Raz.

Uncle Daniel is a Systems Engineer. He lives in Nashville, Tennessee, with his wife, his son, and his Corgi named Raz.

When Uncle Daniel was young he enjoyed reading books because he was curious to learn about everything.

Uncle Daniel especially loved learning about science and technology. At that time he didn't know he wanted to be a Systems Engineer. When he was a kid he didn't know the job of Systems Engineer existed.

Uncle Daniel knew that different types of engineering have been important to the modern world. When he was old enough to go to college he decided to study Electrical Engineering. In addition to taking his classes, he worked at a job in software development.

NEVER STOP LEARNING

After graduation, Uncle Daniel interviewed for jobs. One company had a program to train young people just out of college to be Systems Engineers. This turned out to be just the right job for Uncle Daniel.

He learned that the main work of a Systems Engineer was to design computers and software to help people do their jobs better.

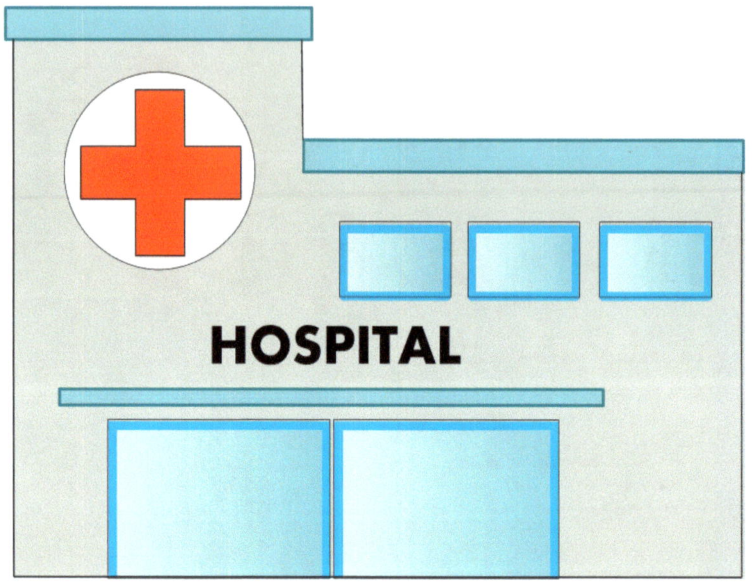

Systems Engineers work in many different types of businesses. Uncle Daniel works in healthcare, so he spends much of his time making improvements in the way hospitals work.

Uncle Daniel spends part of his time meeting people in healthcare to find out how he can help solve their problems. Often they need a new app or service, so Uncle Daniel uses what he knows about technology to help design the computers and software they need.

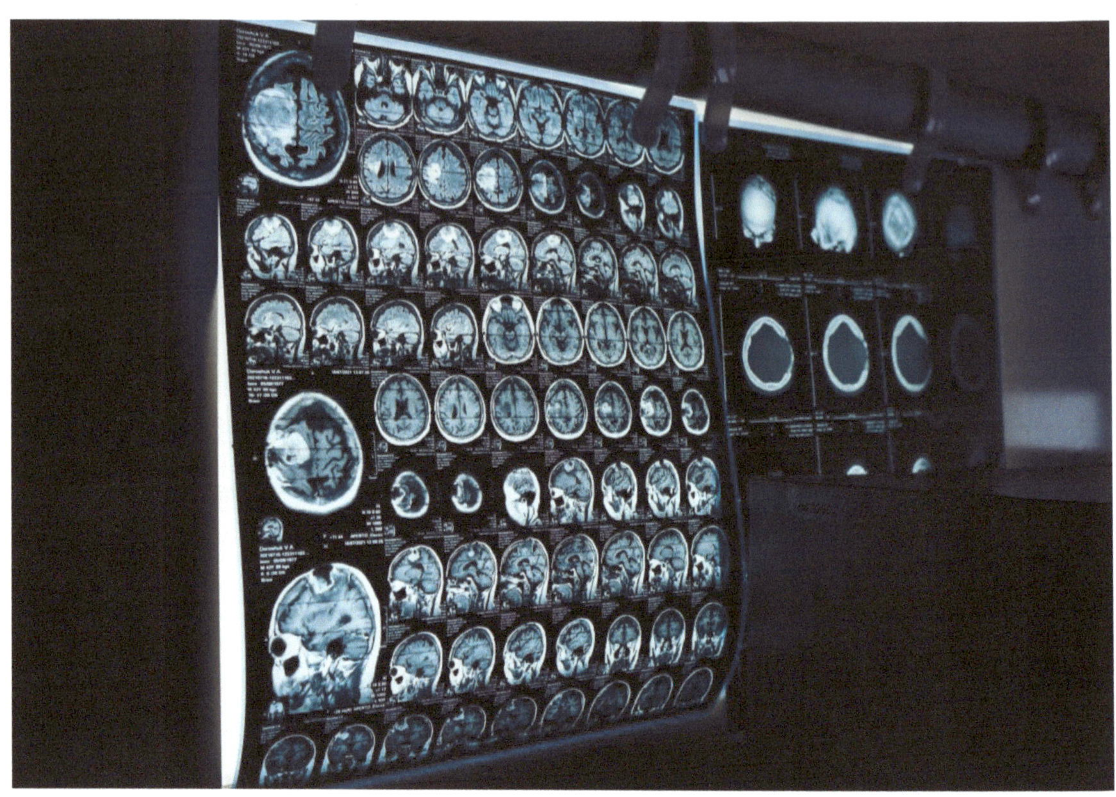

One thing a hospital might need is a better way to digitally store all the patients' X-rays, MRIs, and other images.

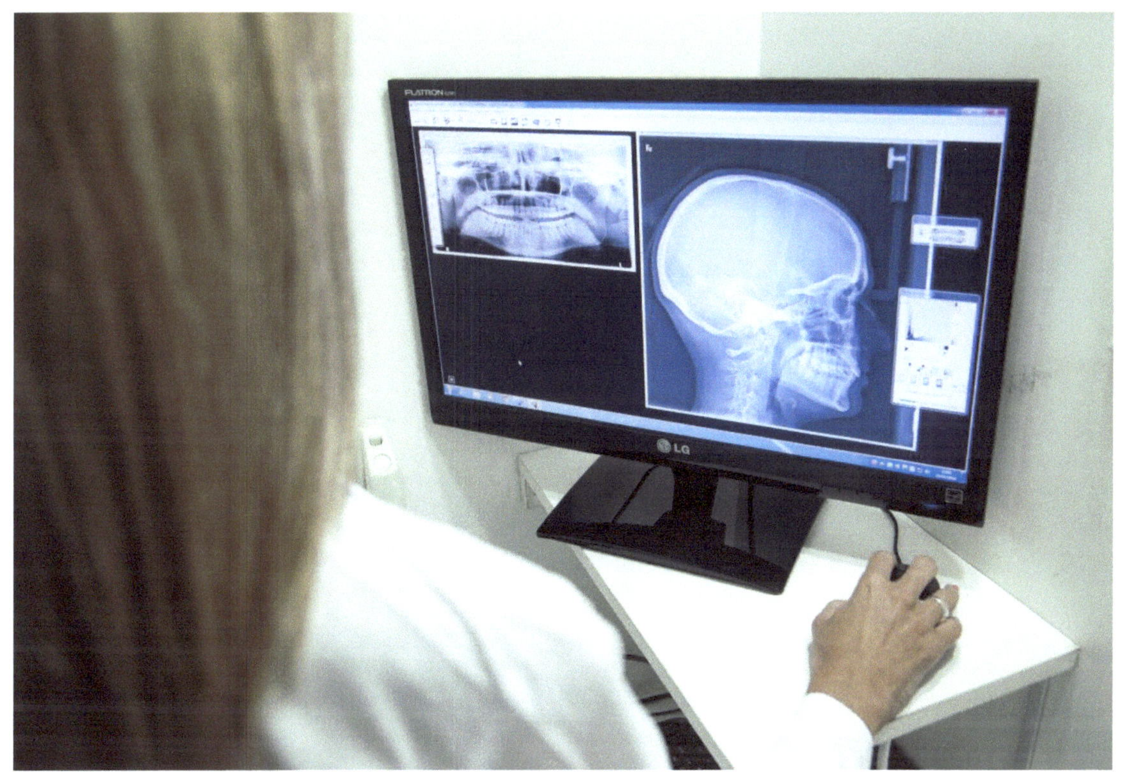

Uncle Daniel must design a system that works fast so that doctors, nurses, and radiologists don't have to wait to see images when treating patients.

The system Uncle Daniel designs must continue to work and to not lose any patient records if a computer breaks or if the power goes out in the city.

Uncle Daniel must plan all the ways to make the computers and software meet the needs of everyone. His job is to think and solve problems before they happen.

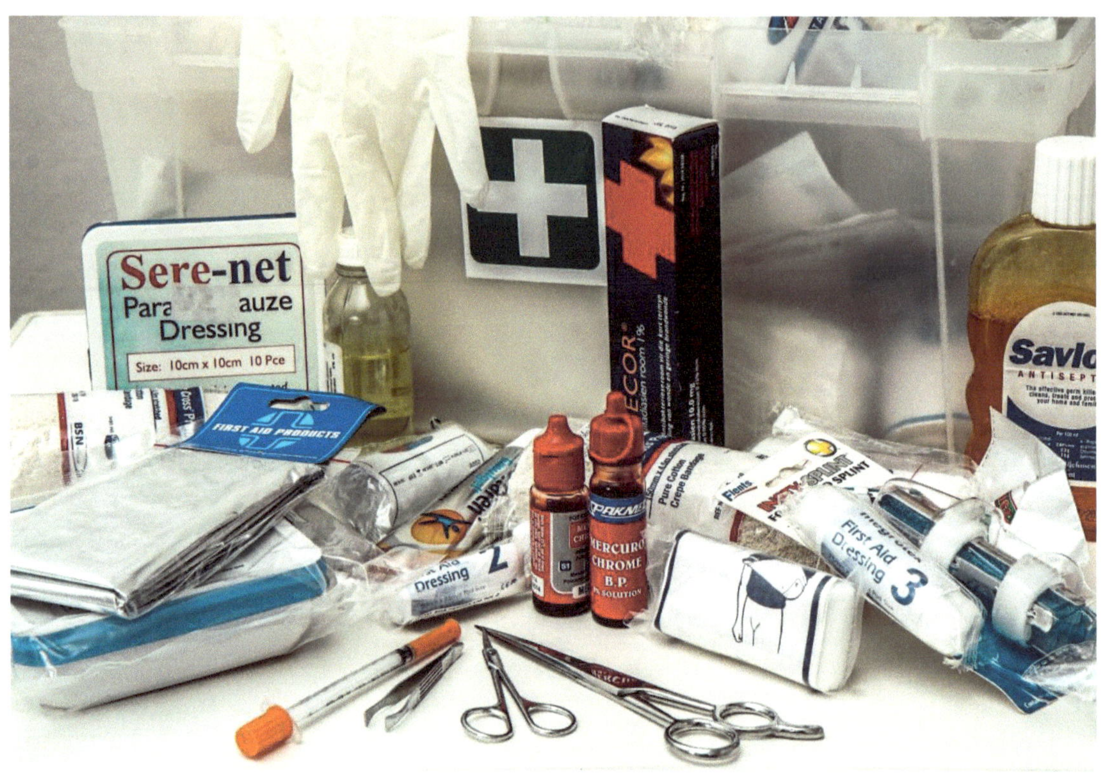

Another way Uncle Daniel helps workers in a hospital is to design systems that help nurses keep track of their supply closets.

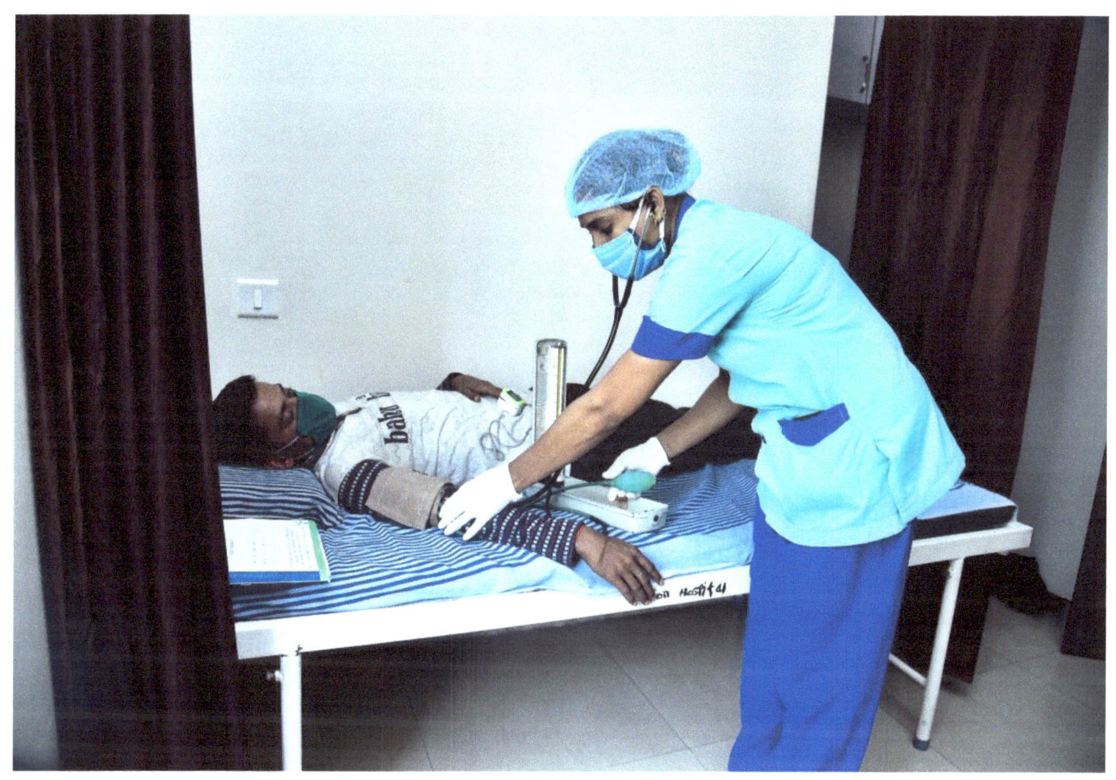

It is important that hospitals do not run out of the supplies used to treat patients every day. They need a computer system that automatically counts how many supplies are used and how many need to be ordered.

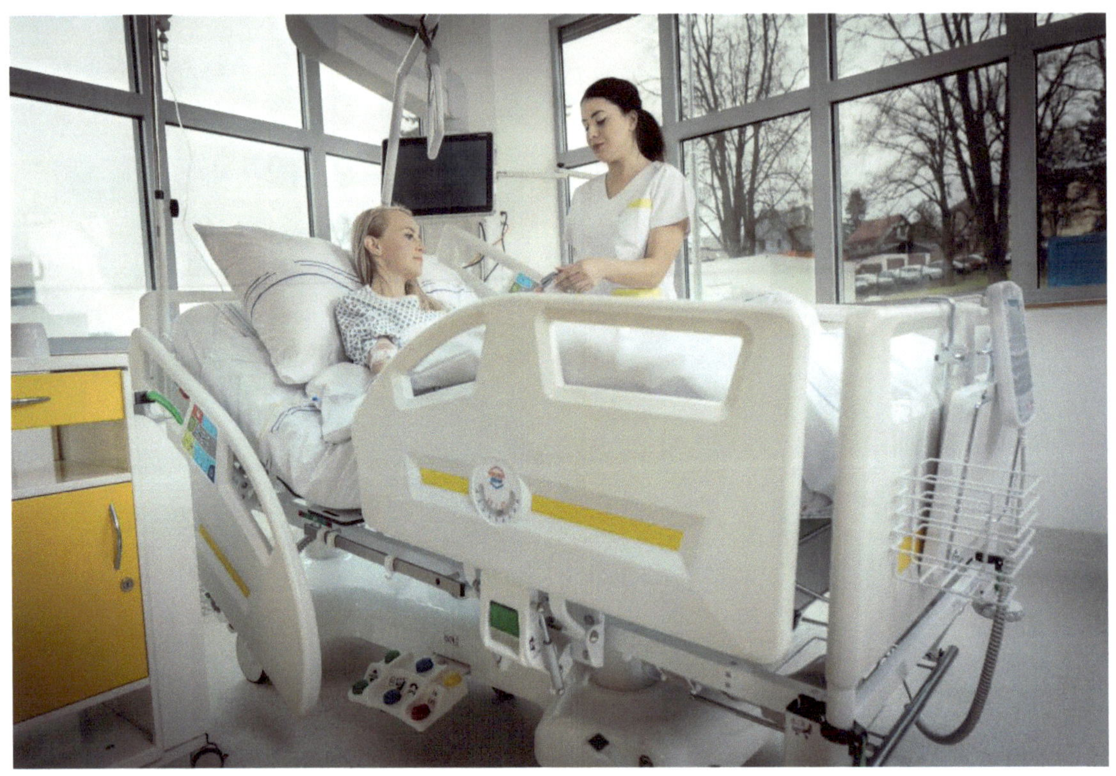

Nurses have more time to take care of patients if they don't have to spend a lot of time counting supplies. Uncle Daniel's work as a Systems Engineer helps patients get better care in the hospital.

A Systems Engineer like Uncle Daniel works with other people to make a project successful. He obtains information from Product Managers when a new system is needed. He also works with IT administrators to make sure new computer systems are set up correctly. He might also consult with Security Engineers to ensure protections are in place to prevent bad guys from breaking into the new computer system.

Good communication skills are an important part of working as a Systems Engineer. Some days Uncle Daniel talks to lawyers while planning his projects.

Computer science is a big field, so Uncle Daniel might consult with another Systems Engineer who is an expert in a different area. Systems Engineers learn from each other by sharing information when there is a problem to solve.

When a project is finished, another part of Uncle Daniel's job is to teach workers how to use the computer systems and software he designs. He shows workers how to use the system to make their work easier, and he answers all their questions.

Uncle Daniel wants kids to know they should always ask questions about how things work. So many things kids see and touch every day were invented by people who were solving problems. Information about how people built things in the past helps us improve and build even better things in the future.

Now that you know about Uncle Daniel and his work, it's time to think about what kind of work you might do when you grow up. Maybe you'll want to do the same kind of work your parents do. Or maybe you'll decide you want to be a Systems Engineer like Uncle Daniel.

Also by Anita Stafford

Picture books
A Vegetable Garden is Not For Cows
Briley Isabelle Gordon Wants a Cat
The Disappearance of Mr. White
Vegetables Smegetables
Hooray Hooray It's Purple Day
We Are Different, We Are the Same
Laughing Ladybug Meets the Grumpy Bugs
If Moms Were Flowers I'd Pick You
Can You See Me Now: Cheetahs Hiding in Plain Sight
The Squirrel School Picnic
My Brother's Allergy: Peanuts

The Career Kids Series
Uncle Philip is a Farmer
Aunt Tiffany is an Artist
Aunt Virginia is a Seamstress
Aunt Kelly is a Realtor

Chapter books
The Sassafras House series including:
The Legend of Sassafras House
Treasure in Catclaw Canyon
The Catnapper Mystery

For adults
Confessions of a Cell Phone Loser

Watch for more at www.anitastafford.com
Don't forget to sign up for the email newsletter on the website!

About the Author

Anita Rowe Stafford makes her home in northeastern Arkansas. She worked in public school for more than twenty years as a teacher and a counselor. Anita has taught students from kindergarten to graduate level, and she is also a Licensed Professional Counselor.